The Satu
Volume 1:
The Love Will Remain

by Paul Grimsley

from *Musehick Publications*

The Saturday Books Volume 1: The Love Remains
Copyright ©2020 Paul Grimsley
Artwork ©2020 Paul Grimsley

ISBN: 978-1-944864-93-4

Musehick Publications
musehickpublications.com

All Rights Reserved.
Any unauthorized copying, translation, duplication, importation or distribution, in whole or in part, by any means, including electronic copying, storage or transmission, is a violation of applicable laws.

To Gandalf

escaping paralysis 7
until you start 9
the rules of the game 10
in the differences 11
devices 12
relax 13
walls between 14
ageing into null 15
inside art 16
forgotten seasons 17
some fragments large 18
the saw us 19
change in layers 20
doesn't taste the same 21
in the skin of stories 22
space translated 23
memory condense 24
held apart 25
the promise 26
twenty 27
locked water 28
the game of another 29
the simplicity of love 30
diluted 31
earn a difference 32
deep perspective 33
the heart of this 34
time to stop 35
taking apart 36
the love will remain 37

escaping paralysis

there are ways they seek to paralyse
by making the facts seems like lies
by confusing them with opinion
over which they hold dominion
by shouting a little louder
than the others in the room

it is under a darker flag
it is with a shadier promise
it is with a voice drowned in money
papery charm, slick as oil
you feel the fallen fruit spoil

in the corner
that you have haunted
and been painted into, you sit
watching the flies gather
watching the vultures hang
like kites above carrion

how do you continue hope
when you are aware of the slippery slope
down which many are willing to slide?
you have to keep the light lit inside
the tide to which you're tied
is one you push and carry
with your own pride and gravity

you have to keep in motion
and the devotion
you hand to momentum
births moments and you invent them
and invoke them continually

so they can try all they want
their words are in a smaller font

until you start

you do not know until you start
what will pull your world apart
is it the direction of your heart?
or is it the cadence of your art?

what will put it back together?
will it be the drift of weather
or will it be the question of whether
you are free or held by tether?

every life has watershed
building inside the empty head
a kingdom where a narrative thread
may live a life and then be bled

we pour it into a tiny cup
some days we don't drink it up
some days we just let it spill
some motion that we seek to kill

other times we set a date
and choose to no longer hibernate
and then we begin to create
a fuller cup and a fuller plates

the rules of the game

i am redrawing of lines
pajamas and impromptu shrines
these are the markers of our times
the distance you must maintain
the place in which you must remain
sometimes it goes against the grain
some people claim to go insane
the things you have to explain
how to wash your hands
how to sanitise
isolation demands

i was pretty much doing it before
sat behind a closed door writing
but now we are amidst a feline war
and the rules of the game are biting

in the differences

who wants to live in the differences?
pushed up against the outside
cool glass, damp concrete
a clammy hand, an unwelcome fingertip

you aren't a fat lip anymore
you aren't a clipped ear
you aren't standing in the corner
with your hands on your head

where you grew up the map was homogeneous
people looked like people looked like people
like paperdolls in a cutout string
the boredom suburbia can bring

some people are bruises
feeling all the abuses
like dropped fruit
windfall fallen further

devices

anchored to glass slabs
hung in the skinned space
tales and data trails
swirling through the helical riptide
pause for the upswing at open nodes

we look up to see other faces
that were glued
blue light hued
that we haven't viewed
unfiltered in years

we hold out a hand
and the flat palm denies
and we step into accepted distance
the atomisation of a social norm

i'm not a backbone pushing
i am not a hand holding
i am a spirit pause

relax

we are comfortable next to each other
duration is not an issue
heartbeat and heat
watching the screen
pre-pandemic streets
we drink coffee
and think about how we wouldn't be doing much else
if we could spend this time together normally
there is just a slight edge under the relax
it's like a hidden tax

walls between

walls between
the door, the screen
the hidden, the seen
what's the scene?

these hands gloved
this face masked
questions asked
philosophies shoved

and some people move along
listening to a different song
like they were never listening to the same tune
reading some mystic rune, visiting from the moon

ageing into null

do you age into different poems?
the anger sapped out of the words?
are you sucking on the muzak teat?
do you feel complete
and done with curiosity?

your words have no threat
you say nothing to politicians
have surrendered the power of art
have laid down the pen
taken up with the wooden sword
sat upon some other hobby-horse

if you aren't alive
don't write
no one needs despatches from the grave

inside art

an artist's eye
detects, disassembles
makes flat shapes that resemble
the world we wander through
an artist's eye reframes the view

i come form Constable country
it still looks the same
is worthy of the name
we hang in that frame
out by Flatford Mill

i remember walking through there
fully aware i was inside art
that the tide were lapping through my heart
and the world and painting would never be apart
from that moment forward

forgotten seasons

i have forgotten seasons
baked into florida same
a different kind of game
fall happens elsewhere
we have blip-winters
we have downpours
but mostly we have sun
i recall some of the smells
sense memory deepens the picture
but autumn never troubles the path
just ticking lizards
pollen instead of cuckoos for spring
different levels of being baked
talk of august
but no one really buys that the seasons shift
so the clock changes twice a year annoy

some fragments large

i watch the eighties crystallise
and wonder at the distance between then and now
the nineties were significant
but who likes to freeze anywhere
fuck the generational labels
and the two thousands, what were they?
personal insight aside, what were they?

you edge out of ages sideways
like trying to pass in a narrow corridor
do you think of it in terms of comedy?
music? Television

all opinions come from dead comics
and old films
and misremembered lyrics
epic poems in the hopper
Hopper on the wall
some fragments large, some small

typewriters, abacus, notepads
there is dust on my formative influences
so i shake it off, move on
wait for the echoes to be gone

the saw us

snatching the dictionary
out of another's hands
and telling them their labels
mean something else
they will find in the thesaurus of you
a meeting place of the false and true
just like anywhere else

trying to squash the lies down
can fill us with vinegar
pickle our hopes
all the pickled punks in the nursery
something cursory cursed
that feels like it can't be reversed
but because you know it was rehearsed
can totally be undone
like a shoe
like a fired gun

i'm fresh, new, reborn
you stand there, pages torn

change in layers

am i a chameleon
or an onion?
looking for each omen
playing cards reparsed
hung upside down
a wise man grown in a tree
with money for leaves
a tap hammered in leaking sap
in the tube we mind the gap

some days i decide to be
a dance exercise
a thumbnail sketch
a rube goldberg machine
gargling with salt water

i am matched to the wallpaper
i am glitch art easy disintegration
i am matchbook flare

doesn't taste the same

one more reboot
dulls the shine
the light stutters through shutters
and gutters in the frame
a failing canted flame

we know your name
have played the game
it's played out
become one more drought
you must live through
to achieve growth through pain

a forest of trees bent by wind
fruit on the ground
easy to go with something found
than something brand new
but it doesn't taste the same

in the skin of stories

living in the skin of stories
stacked in the ghost potentialities
where mathematics edges into frameworks
we hang pictures in the caesuras
beetles on their backs pedalling the air

we chew on poems
to sharpen our teeth
preparing for the meat
we have to hunt down
plucking rib cages from our own myth
to feed new myths of another fire

through forests
masks hung in the trees
animals scenting the breeze
sat there, we read
we write
we talk
we translate the world as we walk

space translated

the translated space
the triangulated space
where you find yourself
and paint your face

a hand pressed to the mirror
grease
moments where the sense of self can cease
walk to the edge of the room
translate a tomb to a loom to a womb

you have the power
to flower more than once a year
to tear a tear
and exalt in the wired weird
and move away from all you've feared
into something close to what you are
inside a bar, outside a car, near and far
when is a door not a door; when it's a jar

memory condense

gathering up into pixels
into scattered lines
into scrapbook memories
into something other
the way we made ourselves had changed
new parts; not hearts rearranged

music is broken collections
melodies that fall out of birds
are put into words and abstract shapes
until we can box the sunlight
and capture the early morning

a pooled afternoon
begins as a mirror
waiting for rain to fill it
cut from a painting
wrapped in tin foil
pressed between books
a dried flower

held apart

magic is two islands
electrical fields held apart
touching
fingertips, lips
and other acreage of skin

sometimes i forget my own body
until saliva is applied
until the boundaries are tried
until proximity is supplied
and then i am more alive

the promise

the promise that is held
is the promise to yourself
nothing to do with what others voice
what others see as the choice
that you must make
the path that is yours to take
unfolds before your feet alone
and the promise is no else's to own
you find a coloured stone
you find an ancient bone
sat in a field learning the world
your bird of books with latin names
all those solitary games
you arrive somewhere others desired
and they get all fired up
because you did well
if you went another way they'd say you failed
so many people by expectations jailed

twenty

the twentieth of anything
in the year of 2020
the time for speculation seems plenty
this is wrong
and that is wrong
and here's a song
to commemorate the failing state

we are fed on bad news
muse upon the fuel fed by the muse
kneeling in fallen leaves
from uninterested trees
wondering what someone believes
this man smiles
this woman grieves
this child is honest
this possum deceives

he comes on
we turn it off
in no way roundabout
barely straightforward
not wanting to bank on hindsight

locked water

collapsed
elapsed
trapped
traipsed
any routine
can make a machine
the robot in us
the desire for program

clasped
elastic
tap
the teeth closed about
time finds brackets
possibility collapsing

a wave
a mirror
an enclosed sea
the hand shocked
the land locked
we are looking out to the horizon

the game of another

the path of one
becomes the game of another
footsteps transmogrified
choreographed dance
it is distanced in time
but the pattern is observable
loaned meaning by a narrative
that slowly accrues
in the words we choose to use
maybe it can be a game for others too

the simplicity of love

how complicated does love need to be?
simplicity unpack
in front of us not behind our backs
and anyone that attacks
is trying to erase their tracks
for something they did wrong

an honest hand
and honest heart
can handle
what tears another apart
where one thing seems to end
one can dream a start

love needs no complication at all
eve and adam need no fall
to explain them
no apology to exculpate them

diluted

we trade ourselves for something else
a lesser goal; a diluted us
the mask sets in
a fixed property of face
the marker of a place

a fingerprint inside a heart
leaves a trace
the tongue dart
inside the mouth
tasting the sweetness of the kiss
the heat

we walk down the street
and we say this is mapped
this is known
this is as grown
as it will ever be
the i sever you
and you sever me

sad stories
or love stories
or no stories
there is nothing else
even with the window dressing

earn a difference

i take sentences
and break sentences
so i can hang other truths
in the hollowed out shell of their sound
the swallowed doubt swells where its found

dictionary bonfire
thesaurus conflagration
the meat of poets
the hearts of artists

there is no thing
that is one way
when viewpoint can touch it
and magic can earn it a difference

deep perspective

some things are not possible
says the person who thinks only of the possible
based upon the solid actual
like the limited future is factual
and curtailed fate is contractual

we can live in a small world
or we can push into the margins
and escape the edge of the page
into something that is a raging sea

we paint deep perspective
for the hunger of the vanishing point
where we all want to disappear to
because it as an horizon dreaming

the heart of this

we do not wish to be in the heart of this
we are seeking peripheries
where they become boundaries
people at a distance
for some they work better that way

we see someone approach
and actions speak louder than words
we cross the street
we do not want to meet
the danger of the meat

the sneeze
something incomplete
everybody will be discreet
leaving no footprint
except a coffee can full of ashes
from someone no-one wanted
to turn into a diamond

time to stop

there are small breakages in him
but they are amplified
his breathing catches
on the jagged edges
and you see him wince
at the corner of the street

he sits there and tries to burn away memories
with the heat of whiskey
a temporary cauterisation
he laughs like a healed man
wakes like a dead man

is she a ghost after maths has failed?
when the day doesn't add up
to more than a bag full of broken parts?
the clocks around the room are broken hearts

taking apart

taking apart the fish he understands life
in its absence

taking apart the clock he understands time
in the stillness

taking apart the poem he understands art
as something that needs a magician

taking apart a relationship he understands nothing
but the obvious loneliness

the love will remain

thinking about my cat
thinking about my dad
death and the distance travelled

sometimes you hold life close
and it cries out in pain
and it tells you it will need to go
and you know

you sleep close
and you look each other in the eyes
and you say your goodbyes
and one of you leaves
and what is left behind is not the same
and for a moment the love feels like pain
but the pain shall pass and the love will remain

Forthcoming Books

For a full list of our existing and forthcoming books please check out Musehick Publications at musehickpublications.com

Made in the USA
Columbia, SC
22 June 2020